Great Genre Writing Lessons

Focused Step-by-Step Lessons, Graphic Organizers,
and Rubrics That Guide Students Through
Each Stage of the Writing Process

by Heather Clayton

SCHOLASTIC
PROFESSIONAL BOOKS

New York • Toronto • London • Auckland • Sydney
Mexico City • New Delhi • Hong Kong • Buenos Aires

To all the special children in my life.

Acknowledgments

Mom and Dad, I thank you for your continuing love and support of my work, and for being proud of me. And to Todd, I am so lucky to have your constant words of encouragement and patience. I love you.

At Rogers Middle School, thank you to my very special friends and colleagues who have been so supportive of every new idea and classroom endeavor. To Elizabeth, you have been one of my greatest teachers. Your thoughtfulness, feedback and friendship made this book possible. To Carol, your ability to listen and be a pillar of support is something I will always treasure. To Melanie, thank you for all of our reflective conversations about children and their writing, you are an inspirational leader. To Mary Lou, your love of children and literacy are what make you so special.

Cover design by Gerald Fuchs
Interior design by Sydney Wright
ISBN 0-439-26724-2

Copyright © 2003 by Heather Clayton
Published by Scholastic Inc.
All rights reserved. Printed in the U.S.A.
6 7 8 9 10   40   09 08 07 06 05

Contents

Using This Book

Welcome to *Great Genre Writing Lessons!*

The ready-to-go lessons in this book cover the following genres: how-to writing, informational reports and essays, personal narratives, fictional narratives, and persuasive writing. For each genre, you'll find a series of step-by-step lessons presented in sequential order and divided into daily components. Each lesson—designed to help students meet the language arts standards—is targeted for 45 minutes to one hour, but if it is more appropriate within the context of your classroom, lessons can be combined, broken down into additional days, or the order may be changed. Several skills may overlap between genres and there are also many opportunities to revisit skills throughout the different kinds of writing presented in the book. (See the International Reading Association/National Council of Teachers of English languge arts standards matrix on page 7.)

The lessons are designed to help you move students through the writing process. It is important to note, however, that it is not always necessary to take the entire process to completion each time, nor does the process need to end at publishing. For instance, mid-year, students may revise and edit pieces that they had completed in the beginning of the school year.

For each genre, there is a set of reproducibles that can be used in a variety of ways. They are referenced in each lesson, and are appropriate to use as overheads, to put on a classroom chart, or to copy for the students. The model pieces might be shown on an overhead at the beginning of each genre unit, then put up and revisited throughout the lessons. Another option is to copy the models for students and have them practice highlighting topic sentences, leads, conclusions, and so on.

In addition, many of the reproducibles are helpful student resources that can be used throughout the school year. I recommend copying some onto bright colored paper so students can store them in a designated folder and pull them out to refer to when writing.

Included in the reproducibles are required revising and editing checklists for each genre. Students are given a concrete set of tasks to complete when revising or editing their writing. Many students need some direct support as to what to do when revisiting a writing piece. These checklists can be modified to meet the needs of the diverse learners in your classroom. Lastly, when evaluating a piece, using the criteria presented in the required revising and editing checklists ensures that students are addressing the relevant skills.

At the end of the book you'll find a reproducible set of writing tools that are appropriate for any genre. Various rubrics (pages 81–85) help students assess their writing. The self-reflection and partner feedback sheets (pages 87–88) can be reproduced for students and used at the end of any writing piece. The goal-setting sheet (page 89) is also appropriate with any genre, and the self-reflection sheet (page 90) helps students to monitor their progress when working to achieve their goals. And, helpful reproducibles such as a proofreading marks sheet (page 92) and a vocabulary-building sheet for independent use (page 93) can be used all year long. Students can complete one "vocabulary web" per day and keep all pages in a folder. All of these resources are designed for flexibility of use—and to help students develop their skills all year long.

Enjoy!

Heather Clayton

The Writing Process

Selecting a Topic:
Students choose their subject.

Pre-writing:
Students prepare to write by generating ideas and gathering information to record on a planning page or graphic organizer. This phase of the process helps the students organize their thinking and prepare to write.

Drafting:
Referring to their pre-writing notes, students turn bits of ideas into complete thoughts and begin to create a piece. Using pencil, skipping lines and using only one side of the paper is helpful. By doing so, students have space to complete revising and editing.

Revising:
Students revisit their first drafts of writing, and make improvements in the style and content of their writing. It's helpful to use a colored pen to see additions to writing.

Editing:
Students proofread their work, paying careful attention to mechanics, sentence structure, paragraphing, and grammar. Editing should also be done in colored ink (using a different color than the one used during the revising process) so that both you and the students are able to make the distinction between the two different phases of the writing process.

Publishing:
Each writer creates a formal, final copy of their work. Published drafts are often done in ink or on a word processor. When handing in a published copy, students should also hand in the work completed during other phases of the writing process.

Peer and/or teacher conferencing, goal setting, and self-reflection:
This work should be ongoing throughout each phase of the writing process.

Connections to the Language Arts Standards

IRA/NCTE Standards	Process	Informational	Personal Narrative	Fictional Narrative	Persuasive
1. Read to build an understanding of texts, acquire new information, and for personal fulfillment.		✓			
2. Read a wide range of genres to build understanding of many dimensions of human experience.		✓			✓
3. Apply a wide range of strategies to interpret, evaluate and appreciate texts.		✓			✓
4. Adjust use of spoken, written and visual language to communicate effectively.	✓	✓	✓	✓	✓
5. Use different writing process elements to communicate.	✓	✓	✓	✓	✓
6. Apply knowledge of language structure, language conventions, and genre to create, critique and discuss texts.		✓	✓	✓	✓
7. Conduct research by generating ideas and questions. Gather, evaluate, and synthesize data from a variety of sources.		✓			✓
8. Create and communicate knowledge by using a variety of technological and informational resources.	✓	✓	✓	✓	✓
9. Develop an understanding of and respect for diversity in language use, patterns and dialects across cultures.	✓	✓	✓	✓	✓
10. Make use of their first language to develop competency in the ELA and develop understanding of content across the curriculum.	✓	✓	✓	✓	✓
11. Participate as knowledgeable, reflective, creative, and critical members of the community.	✓	✓	✓	✓	✓
12. Use spoken, written, and visual language to accomplish their own purposes.	✓	✓	✓	✓	✓

Writing How-To Pieces

Process Writing

Selecting a Topic

Students will be excited about an opportunity to teach something new to a friend or relative! Very often as readers we are reading and following directions.

1. Have students brainstorm times they have had to follow step-by-step instructions. After eliciting student ideas, tell them they will have an opportunity to construct a writing piece in which they explain to someone how to get somewhere, make something, do something or operate something.

2. One of the most difficult steps in writing an explanation can be choosing a topic. Have students list five things they know how to do well and could explain to an audience in writing.

3. Once students have generated their individual lists, they should circulate them around the class, collecting ten more ideas of things their classmates know how to do.

4. After gathering their list, have students highlight their top three choices. For additional topic ideas, share the list on page 12. For homework, they should consider their top choices, then make a topic selection.

Pre-Writing

Once students have chosen their topics, it is time for them to begin the pre-writing phase. Model for the students the importance of every step of their explanation.

1. When beginning to model the pre-writing phase, place a loaf of bread, a jar of peanut butter, a jar of jelly, a knife, a plate and a napkin on a desk or table where all students can see.

2. Ask for volunteers to explain how you will make a peanut butter and jelly sandwich. As students generate ideas, do exactly as they have told you. For example, if a student tells you to put the peanut butter on the bread and you have not yet opened the jar of peanut butter, place the jar itself on a piece of bread. Students will soon realize how specific they need to be!

3. After modeling the sandwich-making process, have students list each of the correct steps on the graphic organizer (page 21). They should use only key words and phrases.

4. Students are now ready to complete their graphic organizer by filling in the rest of the organizer.

Drafting

Prior to beginning their first drafts, students will need to recognize the importance of using transition words to link steps and ideas.

1. Show students a sample recipe from a cookbook and ask them to describe how the author moved between each step in the process. As a class, locate all of the transition words listed in the recipe.

2. To give them practice inserting and using transition words, distribute the transition word list (page 15) and give each student a copy of the transition word cloze passage (page 16). Working with a partner, have students fill in the blanks with appropriate transition words. A completed paragraph can be found on page 17.

3. Share the answers students have selected for the blanks. Then have them revisit their own graphic organizers and insert transition words (and materials) for each step.

4. Before students begin drafting, pass out the model process piece (page 14). Ask for a volunteer to read the piece aloud. Explain that the topic sentence will introduce their subject. Highlight the first topic sentence to model for the students and ask them to identify the topic being introduced.

5. Have students highlight the remaining topic sentences in the piece.

6. Once students understand the importance of writing a topic sentence, they are ready to begin drafting their process piece. In addition to an introduction and conclusion, their piece should include all necessary materials for the task, as well as all of the steps from beginning to end, with transition words in between.

Revising

Once students have finished writing their first drafts, they are ready to begin the revising process. While completing all of the revising lessons, students should also be completing the required revising checklist (page 19).

1. Pair each student with a revising buddy and give each buddy a sticky note.

2. While one partner reads their piece, the second partner is to listen and pretend they are trying to complete the task. Depending on the topics chosen, students may be able to act out the steps in their partner's piece.

3. If there are any major steps or details that have been left out, it is the listening partner's responsibility to write it down on a sticky note and stick the note to their partner's paper.

Revising

Students are now ready to search for places in their piece where they can combine sentences by adding a conjunction. Combining sentences reduces the choppy sounds in their writing.

1. Using the combining sentences strategy (page 18), model for the students how they would read their piece to find places that sound choppy, look for short sentences that can be combined, then combine sentences using a conjunction. It is also important that the students re-read after revising to make sure their writing makes sense.

2. Once you have modeled for the students, give them an opportunity to combine sentences in a practice passage.

3. Students are then ready to revise their own pieces, looking for places where they can add conjunctions.

Editing

Using their required revising and editing checklist (page 19), students edit their piece for correct spelling, capitalization, punctuation, paragraphing and grammar.

Possible Topics for
PROCESS WRITING

- applying nail polish
- sharpening a pencil
- making microwave popcorn
- doing laundry
- making an ice cream sundae
- feeding a pet
- drawing a stick figure
- folding a sweatshirt
- making a glass of lemonade
- doing a jumping jack
- tying a shoe
- making a paper airplane
- solving a simple math problem
- addressing an envelope
- washing dishes
- braiding hair
- making a bed
- vacuuming
- changing a light bulb
- using the dishwasher
- checking out a library book
- making a sandwich
- putting in earrings
- applying lip gloss

Peer Conferencing

Prior to writing the final copy of their process piece, students should share pieces with a peer and elicit feedback (page 20 or 85).

Publishing

Students are now ready to publish their final copy. As a follow-up, students can give oral presentations, modeling for the class the steps presented in their process piece. After publishing, students can self-reflect on their work and set goals for their work in this genre (pages 86 and 87).

Additional Ideas for Teaching
PROCESS WRITING

- Give pairs of students copies of how-to books, cookbooks, craft books, and so on, and have them select a section, read it together and list any of the transition words they find. Use student findings to create a large class transition word list.

- For a warm-up exercise, post a topic on the board and have the students explain the process in an expository paragraph in their journals. Topics may include tying a shoe, brushing teeth, combing hair, preparing a bowl of cereal, and so on.

- Run off sheets of step-by-step directions for simple tasks. Cut up the sheets and keep them in plastic bags. When students finish work early they can practice sequencing by spilling out the steps and putting them in sequential order.

- When reading or completing work in other curriculum areas, have the students be "transition word detectives" and keep an ongoing list of any transition words they encounter.

- Have students create and illustrate flipbooks describing the steps to completing a task.

How to Make Toast

Have you ever craved a crunchy treat to complement your scrambled eggs? Warm buttered toast is a snap if you follow these easy instructions.

To begin, make sure you have all of the appropriate supplies. You will need: fresh bread (any kind), a toaster, a knife, a plate or napkin, and a topping of your choice (butter, margarine, cinnamon and sugar, or jam). First, open the bag of bread. Once you have decided how many pieces you would like to toast, insert them into the slots in the toaster. Most importantly, remember to plug in the toaster so it will heat your bread. Before pushing down the lever to start the toasting process, select how darkly toasted you would like your bread to be.

While waiting for your toast to pop up out of the toaster, open any of the toppings you will be adding. Once the toast is ready, carefully remove it from the toaster. Next, place the toasted bread on the plate or napkin. Then, using the knife, spread the topping of your choice onto your toast. Enjoy eating your delicious toast alone or with another yummy dish!

Lastly, close up any open packages and unplug the toaster so that it may cool. It is also important to clean up your work space. Remember these easy directions any time you crave a delicious snack!

Great Genre Writing Lessons Scholastic Professional Books

Transition Words and Phrases

accordingly	for instance	nevertheless
after	for one thing	next
after that	for this reason	now
afterward	furthermore	one
also	hence	once
another	however	on the contrary
as a result	I feel that	on the other hand
as an example of	in addition	on the whole
as proof	in conclusion	or
as soon as	in short	other
at first	in spite of	otherwise
at last	instead	similarly
at the same time	in my opinion	soon
before long	in other words	specifically
besides	in the first place	still
consequently	in the meantime	that is
earlier	in the same way	then
even if	it is my belief that	therefore
even so	later	to begin with
eventually	likewise	to illustrate
finally	meanwhile	thus
first, second, third	moreover	when
for example	most importantly	yet

Great Genre Writing Lessons Scholastic Professional Books

Brushing Your Teeth

Keeping your teeth healthy is a snap if you know how to brush them correctly. _____, you will need a toothbrush with soft or hard bristles, a sink with running water, a cup, and a towel.

_____, place your toothbrush under the water to get the head or top of it wet. The water may be warm or cold depending on the sensitivity of your teeth. _____, squeeze a half-inch long squirt of toothpaste onto the bristles of your toothbrush.

_____ applying the toothpaste, gently place the tooth-brush into your mouth. Place the brush so the bristles are against your teeth and brush in a circular motion. _____, remember to polish top and bottom teeth in the front and back of your mouth.

_____ you have brushed for at least three minutes, expectorate or spit out the extra toothpaste that is in your mouth into the sink. _____ fill the cup with water of any temperature and rinse out your mouth. _____ you will be ready to spit again. _____ wipe your mouth dry with the towel and put all of your materials away. _____ of your hard work, you will have sparkling white teeth!

Great Genre Writing Lessons Scholastic Professional Books

Key

Brushing Your Teeth

Keeping your teeth healthy is a snap if you know how to brush them correctly. To begin, you will need a toothbrush with soft or hard bristles, a sink with running water, a cup, and a towel. First, place your toothbrush under the water to get the head or top of it wet. The water may be warm or cold depending on the sensitivity of your teeth. Next, squeeze a half-inch long squirt of toothpaste onto the bristles of your toothbrush. After applying the toothpaste, gently place the toothbrush into your mouth. Place the brush so the bristles are against your teeth and brush in a circular motion. While brushing, remember to polish top and bottom teeth in the front and back of your mouth.

Once you have brushed for at least three minutes, expectorate or spit out the extra toothpaste that is in your mouth into the sink. Now fill the cup with water of any temperature and rinse out your mouth. Before long you will be ready to spit again. After that, wipe your mouth dry with the towel and put all of your materials away. As a result of your hard work, you will have sparkling white teeth!

Great Genre Writing Lessons Scholastic Professional Books

Combining Sentences

❀ Two short sentences can be joined to make one longer sentence.

❀ A comma and a conjunction are used to join them.

❀ Some conjunctions are:

and	or	so
but	for	yet

When revising . . .

1. Read your piece to find any spots that sound "choppy."

2. Look for any short sentences that can be combined.

   example: *Take the bread. Take the plate.*

3. Decide on which conjunction should be used to combine the sentences. Combine the sentences by using a conjunction, and adding a comma and/or other words if necessary.

   example: *Take the bread **and** put it on the plate.*

4. Read to see if the sentence makes sense!

Great Genre Writing Lessons Scholastic Professional Books

Process Writing

Required Revising

1. ____ Highlight your TOPIC SENTENCE that introduces your subject. If you haven't included a topic sentence, add one.

2. ____ Draw a box around the MATERIALS needed and number the STEPS in your piece. All necessary materials and steps should be listed, and be in sequential order.

3. ____ Circle each TRANSITION WORD you have used. Add a minimum of 2 additional transition words to your piece.

4. ____ Draw a line under any of the places in your piece that sound choppy. COMBINE SENTENCES in a minimum of 2 places in your piece using a conjunction.

5. ____ Highlight your CONCLUSION to check for closure to the piece.

Required Editing

1. ____ Circle a minimum of 3 words with questionable spellings. Look up the correct spelling in the dictionary and write it above the word.

2. ____ Put a dot under the first word in each sentence to be sure you have used a capital letter. Add capital letters where they are needed.

3. ____ Draw a box around the punctuation at the end of each sentence. Make sure you have used the appropriate punctuation.

Great Genre Writing Lessons Scholastic Professional Books

Questions to guide listening for PROCESS PIECES:

Title: _____

Author: _____ Listener: _____

1. What is the topic of the process piece?

   _____

2. Has the author included all of the necessary steps to complete the
   task described in the piece?

   _____

3. Is the information presented in sequential order?

   _____

4. Has the author included transition words?

   _____

5. Are you left with any questions at the end of the piece?
   If so, what are they?

   _____

   _____

   _____

   _____

   _____

   _____

Great Genre Writing Lessons Scholastic Professional Books

Graphic Organizer for Process Writing

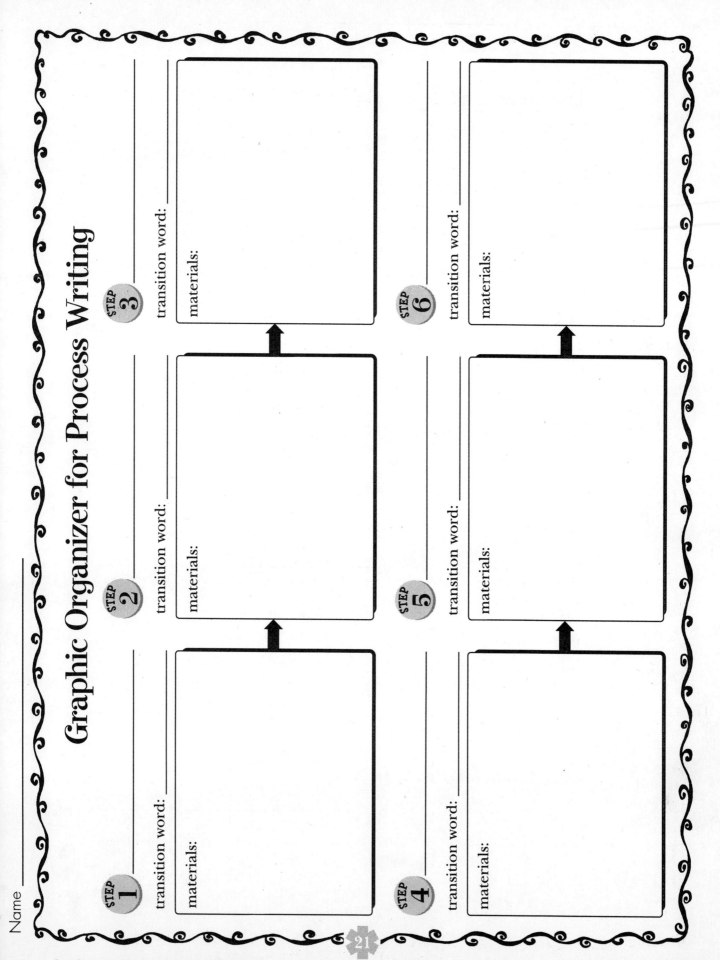

STEP 1

transition word: _____

materials: _____

STEP 2

transition word: _____

materials: _____

STEP 3

transition word: _____

materials: _____

STEP 4

transition word: _____

materials: _____

STEP 5

transition word: _____

materials: _____

STEP 6

transition word: _____

materials: _____

Great Genre Writing Lessons Scholastic Professional Books

Writing Radical Reports and Essays!

Informational Writing

Selecting a Topic

Choosing just the right topic will motivate students to research and gather interesting information for their essays or reports. You might have students choose from a specific list of topics, or have them select their own original topics. Either way, students should feel they have some choice about the topic they will be researching.

1. Have students make a "Top 5" list from an already established topics list (create one based on your curriculum).

2. Place students' names into a hat. As you draw names from the hat, students choose a topic from their "Top 5" list. If one of their choices is already taken, students can choose another option from their list.

3. Students may also choose their own topics from within an already established theme, or possibly choose anything they wish to research. When guiding students in selecting a topic, remind them that the topic should be both interesting and specific.

4. Share a model informational report (page 31) to familarize students with the genre.

Pre-Writing (a)

1. Once students have chosen their topics, they can prepare to gather information. In either a web, a K-W-L chart (page 29), or a list, have students brainstorm specific questions they have about the topic.

2. Next, students should group their questions into subtopics. For instance, if researching a state in the United States, a student may take a question about where the state is located, together with a question about how large the state is, and group them both into the subtopic of geography. Other subtopics for this example could include economy, people, and attractions.

3. In addition to the questions students formulate *before* researching, they will identify additional questions on their own as they gather new information. Encourage this independent questioning process—it is very important to the research phase.

Pre-Writing (b) ....

Students need a place to put the information they gather in their research, and notecards are easy to manage. Encourage students to color-code their notecards by subtopic. This will help them to know where to write the information they find, and how to gather it together when they are preparing to write their essays or reports.

1. Modeling how to take notes on a notecard is helpful. Using a short non-fiction passage, explore with students possible subtopics and research questions. Give students several notecards each, in a variety of colors. Have them label each of their cards with a different subtopic.

2. As you read the passage aloud, have students write important key words and phrases on the appropriate notecard. Remind them to leave ample space between each line, and emphasize the importance of writing neatly so the information gathered is legible.

3. Remind students to record their sources on each notecard so they can give proper credit in the bibliography. Teach them to assign a number, letter or symbol to each source so they don't need to write lengthy author and title information on each notecard.

Pre-Writing (c) ....

1. After gathering all of their research information, students should divide their notecards into categories or subtopics. (The color coding makes this simple.)

2. Advise students to make sure that every subtopic has a title. Explain that these subtopics will represent each of the different paragraphs in the essay or report, as well as an introduction and conclusion.

3. Show students how to translate their subtopic notecards—details only—into an outline (page 30). Explain that TS stands for topic sentence, D stands for detail(s), and CS stands for closing sentence.

Pre-Writing (d)

After putting the *details* into their outlines, students will identify their topic and closing sentences. The structure of the outline will help students write organized paragraphs during the drafting phase.

1. Explain that the topic sentence sits at the beginning of the paragraph and states what the paragraph is about. A good topic sentence is clear and interesting, and includes two main parts: the subject (who or what the paragraph is about) and the focus (what the paragraph is going to say about the subject). Use page 32 to teach about topic sentences.

2. Teach students that the closing sentence summarizes the information in the paragraph, leaves the reader feeling the idea is complete, and provides a transition into the next paragraph. Provide students with models and have them practice writing their own closing sentences.

Drafting

As you prepare students to begin the first drafts of their essays or reports, introduce them to the importance of a powerful introduction.

1. Read the following examples aloud and discuss why they would probably not be effective in gaining the reader's attention.

   "In my report I will tell you about _____."

   "This essay is about _____."

   "Now I will tell you about _____."

   "Listen carefully as you learn about _____."

2. Explore with students the process of writing an engaging introduction. Play with using an interesting quote, a dramatic statement, or a vivid description. Remind students that their introductions should introduce the character or subject as well as briefly mention each of the subtopics that will be covered in the reports. Students should complete the introduction portions of their outlines before writing introductions in their first drafts.

3 Next, guide students through developing the outlines and then the first drafts of their body paragraphs and conclusions. The conclusion should end the report with a strong point as well as a summary of the information presented.

Revising

Give students time to revise their own writing using the required revising checklist (page 33).

Editing

On the required editing checklist, have students edit their essays or reports for correct spelling, capitalization, punctuation, paragraphing, and grammar.

Peer Conferencing

Prior to writing final copies of their essays or reports, students should share their written pieces with each other and elicit feedback (pages 35 or 85).

Publishing and Final Bibliography

Students are now ready to publish their final copies, which include bibliography pages listing the materials and resources used to write their reports or essays. Once the entire writing process has been completed, students should reflect and set goals with regards to their strengths and needs as researchers and informational writers (pages 34 and 86).

Suggested Bibliography Format

Books: Author's last name and first name. <u>Title</u>. City: Publisher, copyright date.

Magazines: Author's last name and first name. "Title of the Article." <u>Title</u>, date: page numbers.

Encyclopedias: "Title." <u>Title of encyclopedia</u>. Edition or version. Other (CD-Rom). Date.

Internet: Author <e-mail address>. "Post title." <u>Site title</u>. Post date. Site sponsor. Date accessed. <Electronic address>.

Name _____

K
What I *know* about my topic

W
What I *want to know* about my topic

L
What I *learned* as a result of my research

Great Genre Writing Lessons Scholastic Professional Books

Informational Writing Outline

Introduction

TS: _____

_____

D: _____

D: _____

D: _____

CS: _____

Body Paragraph

TS: _____

_____

D: _____

D: _____

D: _____

CS: _____

Body Paragraph

TS: _____

_____

D: _____

D: _____

D: _____

CS: _____

Body Paragraph

TS: _____

_____

D: _____

D: _____

D: _____

CS: _____

Great Genre Writing Lessons Scholastic Professional Books

Model Informational Report

West Virginia, "The Mountain State," is a captivating area of the United States with interesting land forms, a pleasant climate, an economy rich in natural resources, intriguing people, and a deep historical background. West Virginia was originally part of the state of Virginia, but became its own state as issues of slavery and economy separated east from west.

West Virginia is bordered by five states—Ohio, Kentucky, Virginia, Maryland, and Pennsylvania—and is home to three geographical regions. The first is the Appalachian Ridge and Valley, which contains the tallest mountains in the state, the Alleghenies. The next, and most heavily populated, is the Appalachian Plateau, covering 80% of the state and plentiful in such natural resources as coal, oil, natural gas, salt, clay, sand, and gravel. The third region is the Blue Ridge, blessed with an abundance of rich soil.

The climate in West Virginia is hospitable with warm summers and mild winters. The average high temperature in July is 87° F while the average low temperature in January is 27° F. Although rare, the state sometimes sees weather extremes as temperatures can climb to a sweltering 114° F or plunge to a frigid -37° F.

West Virginia's abundance of natural resources allows its economy to thrive. While the mountains make for poor farming, the coal, natural gas, salt, clay, and gravel found beneath them are ample compensation. The lush forests that cover the state are also crucial to the economy. Prevailing industries and occupations include coal mining, lumber, chemicals and steel. Chemical and steel factories produce such items as fine glass, bottles, plate glass, dyes, detergents, paints, and plastics. Service industries are also predominant, employing 68% of the state and including tourism, wholesale and retail trade, banking, insurance, and real estate.

West Virginia's 1,800,000 residents are loyal, hard working, and are from a variety of backgrounds including English and German as well as Italian and Irish. The state is primarily White (96%) with a small percentage of African Americans (3%) and Hispanics (1%). Most West Virginians live in rural areas, particularly small coal mining towns. Charleston, the state's capital, is the largest city, with Wheeling, the steel mill center, and Huntington following close behind.

West Virginia offers tourists a plethora of attractions. Harper's Ferry National Historical Park, where the Potomac River meets the Shenandoah, is a captivating reminder of where Robert Harper established his ferryboat business. Tourists can snap postcard-like photographs of the scenic woodlands at the Lost River State Park. Oglebay Park is another must see—a large municipal park with golf courses, indoor and outdoor pools, and even a zoo!

Nestled in the Appalachian Highlands, West Virginia is a beautiful and rugged state blanketed with mountains, rivers, and forests. Tourists visit for the spectacular landscape and the historical attractions. But the Mountain State is home to hard-working, nature-loving people who enjoy plentiful natural resources and thriving industry.

Sample Topic Sentence Activity

Below you will find models of exemplary topic sentences for a historical figure report. On the lines below each topic sentence, create an additional 2 topic sentences to use when writing the first draft of your report.

1. Paul Revere grew up in Boston, Massachusetts, with his nine brothers and sisters.

   • _____
     _____

   • _____
     _____

2. When Paul was a teenager, he had many responsibilities to keep him busy.

   • _____
     _____

   • _____
     _____

3. Paul's adult years were also filled with work and responsibility.

   • _____
     _____

   • _____
     _____

4. Paul Revere was best known for the role he played in the American Revolution.

   • _____
     _____

   • _____
     _____

Great Genre Writing Lessons Scholastic Professional Books

Informational Writing

Required Revising

1 ____ In your INTRODUCTION, **underline** the words that introduce the subtopics to be covered in your essay or report. Draw a squiggly line under the interesting facts used to hook the reader.

2 ____ **Highlight** the TOPIC SENTENCE in each body paragraph. Make sure each topic sentence contains the subject and focus of the paragraph.

3 ____ **Read** each BODY PARAGRAPH in your report. Make sure the details in the paragraph are in logical order and organized. **Add** a minimum of 2 transition words to each paragraph.

4 ____ Place **parentheses** around the CONCLUSION. The conclusion should tie up any loose ends and summarize the information in the essay or report.

5 ____ **Add** more specific details/descriptions in at least 2 different places in your essay or report.

Required Editing

1 ____ **Circle** a minimum of 6 words with questionable spellings. Look up the correct spelling in the dictionary and write it above the word.

2 ____ **Put a red dot** under all capital letters. Capitalize all names and the first word in each sentence.

3 ____ **Draw a box** around the punctuation at the end of each sentence. Make sure you have used the appropriate punctuation.

4 ____ **Put a star** next to each indented paragraph. There should be indentations for the introduction, each body paragraph, and the conclusion.

Research and Report Reflection

1. What were some of your strengths and weaknesses as a researcher?

_____

_____

_____

_____

_____

_____

_____

2. Which stage of the writing process was the easiest? Most difficult? Why?

_____

_____

_____

_____

_____

_____

_____

_____

3. What would you like to improve the next time you write a research report?

_____

_____

_____

_____

_____

4. To make writing a report easier next time, what would you like to learn?

_____

_____

_____

_____

Great Genre Writing Lessons Scholastic Professional Books

Questions to guide listening for REPORTS AND ESSAYS:

Listener: _____

Author: _____ Title: _____

1 What is the topic of the essay or report?

_____

2 Has the author included all of the necessary details to fully explain the topic?

_____

3 Is the information structured clearly? Are the facts presented in sequential order? Has the author included topic sentences?

_____

_____

4 Has the author included a bibliography?

_____

5 What connections can you make to the information presented in the essay or report?

_____

_____

_____

_____

_____

Great Genre Writing Lessons Scholastic Professional Books

Practically Perfect
Personal Pieces!

Personal Narrative Writing

Selecting a Topic

Students enjoy writing about their own experiences—events that made them feel happiness, fear, excitement, or sadness.

1 Have each student fold a sheet of paper into four columns and label each column with the following headings: *experiences with friends and/or family, vacations, lessons I have learned,* and *hobbies.*

2 Under each heading, students should list five descriptors or sentences that match the topic. Some students may need help coming up with ideas (see below).

Pre-Writing

Remind students that when writing about a personal experience, it is important to include all necessary details to make the reader feel as if he/she were there.

1 Begin by using a personal experience of your own as a model, or choose a familiar character in literature and write their personal narrative. Show students how to complete the 6 W's graphic organizer (page 41) by answering who?, what?, where?, when?, why?, and what if?.

2 Next, have students complete the 6 W's graphic organizer for their own topic. By having students complete this organizer before planning the sequence of the details in their piece, their memories will be sharp and they will be more ready to write.

3 Using the same experience and character explored as a class, model the completion of the personal narrative organizer (page 42).

4 Students are now ready to fill in their own personal narrative organizer. Remind them to put themselves at the beginning of the experience. For example, "There I was in the front of our family car . . ." or "I was so excited about an opportunity to go on vacation . . . ."

Possible Topics for

PERSONAL NARRATIVE WRITING

- Describe one of your favorite hobbies.
- Tell a story about a memorable day at school.
- Describe your most frightening experience.
- Write about a time when you felt proud for having accomplished something.
- Describe losing something that was important to you.
- Tell a story about learning to do something that was very difficult for you.
- Share a time when you helped another person or animal.
- Write about a favorite family vacation.
- Describe a time when you felt very nervous.

Drafting (a)

Before students begin their first drafts, share with them an exemplary model of a personal narrative. (Choose one from the curriculum and copy for each student.)

1. Read the narrative aloud and ask students to discuss the strengths of the piece. List their responses.

2. Give each student a copy of the narrative and have them draw brackets around the lead. Point out that an effective *lead* will engage the reader and make them want to finish the story.

3. Read aloud other sample leads from other stories that tell of a person's experience, and encourage students to imitate different authors' styles when crafting their own story leads.

4. Once students have heard a variety of leads, they are ready to write their own. Have them write 2–3 practice leads on separate sheets of paper, putting themselves at the beginning of the experience, and introducing the experience they will describe in their story.

5. Have students share their leads with a partner and elicit feedback as to which lead would be the best to use in their piece.

Drafting (b)

Once students have finished writing their leads, they are ready to continue with the details of their story in sequential order.

1. Supply students with a list of transition words (page 15) and encourage them to use transitions between the details of their story. Have them describe in writing what happened first, second, third, and so on.

2. Now teach students that their conclusions should wrap up the events of their story. Have students draft their own closings.

Revising (a)

Students are likely to have included dialogue in their stories. Use this opportunity to teach them the different dialogue rules.

1. Read through the dialogue rules on page 43 together.

2. Rewrite the passage as a class. Then provide additional passages for students to revise on their own using the correct dialogue rules.

3. Now students will be able to revise the dialogue in their own stories.

Revising (b)

Once they are using dialogue correctly, teach students to use descriptive language in their revisions to engage the reader. Descriptive language gives the reader the experience of feeling what the author felt, using both sensory and concrete details to show—not just tell—the story.

1. Read aloud descriptive excerpts from literature, providing a "tell" sentence before sharing how the author "showed" the reader instead. Distribute pages 44 and 45 and have students read and complete.

2. Arrange desks into five small groups, and at each group post a tent card displaying one of the five senses. Provide things for each student to experience and write about at each of the five senses stations, such as oranges for students to smell; chocolate and caramel for students to taste; music for students to hear; disguised containers of wet, cooked spaghetti for students to feel; and a picture of a beautiful scene for students to see.

3. Provide paper and "tell" sentences (page 46) describing the items at each station. Have students explore the items, and then revise the "tell" sentences into several possible "show" sentences.

4. Have students rotate through the stations and write their own "show" sentences at each. Then ask students to share their responses.

5. Now tell students that another way to "show" something is to replace boring words with juicy ones. Present a list of "boring" vocabulary words such as *said, big, bad,* and *great.*

6. Divide students into teams and have them brainstorm "juicy" synonyms to replace these boring words. Alternatives might be found in the thesaurus, in literature, or in students' own experiences. Distribute page 48 at the end of this exercise.

Revising (c)

Ask students to revise their own writing using the required revising checklist (page 48) as well as their synonym sheets.

Editing

Students are now ready to edit their narratives for correct spelling, capitalization, punctuation, paragraphing, and grammar using their required editing checklist (page 48).

Peer Conferencing

Before they prepare final copies of their personal narratives, encourage students to share their stories with a peer and elicit feedback (pages 49 and 85).

Publishing

Students are now ready to create a formal, final copy of their work. Then guide them through self-reflecting and setting goals for their future narrative writing (page 86).

As a follow-up, students may want to pair up with a peer or younger buddy from another class and share their stories. You might also publish personal narratives to bind into a class book.

Additional Ideas for Teaching
PERSONAL NARRATIVE WRITING

- Type up passages with a number of repetitive, boring words. Have students highlight all of the undesirable words and substitute them with a juicy synonym. You might also ask students to highlight each instance of the word "I" in their own writing, and challenge them to find alternatives.

- For a classroom warm-up exercise, post a "tell" sentence on the board and have students turn it into 3–4 sentences that "show" the reader instead. Some examples could include:
    The popcorn smells delicious.
    The park was pretty.
    The cookies taste good.

- Post pictures with two or more characters together. Have students write a possible dialogue between the characters.

- Provide written conversations that have not followed the dialogue rules and challenge students to edit them.

Name _____

The 6 W's

What?

Who?

Where?

TOPIC

What if?

When?

Why?

Great Genre Writing Lessons Scholastic Professional Books

Name _____

Personal Narrative Organizer

Lead (introductory sentence) _____
_____
_____
_____

Events in sequence

1. _____
_____
_____

2. _____
_____
_____

3. _____
_____
_____

4. _____
_____
_____

Conclusion _____
_____
_____
_____

Great Genre Writing Lessons * Scholastic Professional Books

Name _____

Practice Dialogue Passage

Place quotation marks (" ") only around what a character SAYS.

Use a capital letter after <u>beginning</u> quotation marks (").

Insert punctuation (. , ? !) before <u>ending</u> quotation marks (").

Use juicy words instead of "said" to tell who is talking.

Indent for a new paragraph each time the speaker changes.

Rewrite the following conversation on the lines below.

Hello, Randy said John. How has your day been going? Not so great. I lost my assignment planner and ripped my homework folder. It sounds to me like you will have to make a trip to the bookstore tomorrow morning. How do you keep your papers so organized and your folder so neat said Randy. Well, I clean out my homework folder at least once a week. Don't worry, you'll get the hang of it. I certainly hope so. Thanks for the great advice, said Randy.

_____

_____

_____

_____

_____

_____

_____

_____

_____

_____

_____

_____

Great Genre Writing Lessons Scholastic Professional Books

Show Not Tell

Authors create vivid images in our minds by using words and language that appeal to our senses. For example, an author may include many descriptive adjectives, exciting verbs, and juicy dialogue.

Here are examples from the novel *Island of the Blue Dolphins* by Scott O'Dell.

Example: (Page 1)

Tell: A red ship came to our island.

Show: I remember the day the Aleut ship came to our island.
At first it seemed like a small shell afloat on the sea.
Then it grew larger and was a gull with folded wings.
At last in the rising sun it became what it really was—
a red ship with two red sails.

Example: (Page 42)

Tell: The wild dogs came that night.

Show: The wild dogs came again that night. Drawn by the
scent of fish, they sat on the hill, barking and growling
at each other. I could see the light from the fire
shining in their eyes.

Great Genre Writing Lessons Scholastic Professional Books

Show Not Tell

Great authors use words to paint pictures. They show readers what they mean by using descriptions of how things look, feel, taste, sound, and smell. Rather than **telling** readers that a small child is hungry, an author may *show* it by writing:

The infant's face was a cherry red as he thrashed around in his highchair. He was waiting for the first delicious bite of baby food.

Practice showing (**not telling**) by revising the following sentences:

1 **Tell:** My mother packed some things to take on our vacation.

   Show: _____

   _____

   _____

2 **Tell:** The pizza tasted good.

   Show: _____

   _____

   _____

3 **Tell:** The new car looked nice.

   Show: _____

   _____

   _____

4 **Tell:** I found a pretty rock.

   Show: _____

   _____

   _____

Great Genre Writing Lessons Scholastic Professional Books

Show Not Tell

1. **Tell:** The necklace looked pretty.

   Show: _____

   _____

   _____

   _____

2. **Tell:** The orange smelled good.

   Show: _____

   _____

   _____

   _____

3. **Tell:** The candy tasted great.

   Show: _____

   _____

   _____

   _____

4. **Tell:** I felt something disgusting.

   Show: _____

   _____

   _____

   _____

5. **Tell:** The music sounded exciting.

   Show: _____

   _____

   _____

   _____

Great Genre Writing Lessons Scholastic Professional Books

Sparkling Synonym Sheet

Bad: ghastly, rank, foul, despicable, detestable, obnoxious, heinous, gross, dismal, deplorable, putrid, sinister, wrong, outrageous, atrocious, horrible, nasty, cross, unpleasant, disagreeable, unsuitable, inappropriate, improper, faulty, imperfect, inferior, defective, unfavorable, harmful, spoiled, tainted, contaminated, rotten, wicked, evil, dangerous, vicious

Beautiful: pretty, lovely, handsome, attractive, gorgeous, dazzling, splendid, magnificent, ravishing, graceful, elegant, fine, exquisite, pleasing, shapely, delicate, stunning, glorious, heavenly, radiant, glowing, sparkling

Big: substantial, mammoth, astronomical, ample, broad, expansive, spacious, stout, tremendous, titanic, mountainous, enormous, huge, immense, gigantic, vast, colossal, gargantuan, large, sizeable, grand, great, tall

Good: excellent, fine, respectable, superb, grand, top-notch, first-rate, worthy, noble, great, splendid, beneficial, superior, wonderful, marvelous, suited, suitable, proper, capable, generous, kindly, friendly, gracious, pleasant, agreeable, pleasurable, satisfactory, well-behaved, obedient, honorable, reliable, trustworthy, favorable, profitable, advantageous, righteous, helpful, genuine, ample

Great: noteworthy, worthy, distinguished, mighty, much, powerful, considerable, grand, remarkable

Happy: pleased, overjoyed, content, satisfied, delighted, elated, joyful, cheerful, ecstatic, jubilant, tickled, gratified, glad, grateful, blissful

Hot: scalding, boiling, smoking, smoldering, stolen, scorching, burning, flaming

Important: necessary, vital, critical, indispensable, valuable, essential, significant, primary, considerable, famous, distinguished, notable, well-known

Interesting: fascinating, engaging, sharp, keen, bright, intelligent, animated, spirited, attractive, inviting, intriguing, provocative, thought-provoking, challenging, inspiring, moving, tantalizing, exciting, entertaining, lively, racy, spicy, engrossing, absorbing, consuming, gripping, arresting, enthralling, spellbinding, captivating, enchanting, bewitching, appealing

Little: tiny, small, shrimp, runt, miniature, puny, dinky, limited, itty-bitty, teeny-weeny, microscopic, slight, petite, minute

Mad: furious, angry, enraged, indignant, inflamed, peeved

Old: feeble, frail, ancient, aged, used, obsolete, stale, musty, archaic, traditional, primitive, mature, veteran, out-dated, old-fashioned, broken-down, faded, ragged, dilapidated, worn

Sad: unhappy, miserable, depressed, uncomfortable, wretched, heartbroken, unfortunate, downhearted, sorrowful, dejected, melancholy, glum, gloomy, dismal, discouraged

Scared: afraid, frightened, alarmed, terrified, panicked, fearful, insecure, timid, shy, skittish, jumpy, disquieted, worried, troubled, disturbed, horrified, apprehensive, petrified, shocked

Great Genre Writing Lessons Scholastic Professional Books

Personal Narrative

Required Revising

1. ____ **Select** a minimum of 2 sentences in your piece and make them "show," not "tell." One of the sentences should come from your lead.

2. ____ **Replace** a minimum of 4 words with a "juicy" synonym.

3. ____ **Add dialogue** to your piece to *apply* your understanding of the dialogue rules. If you have already used dialogue, add 1 more sentence to the conversation and remember to use "said" words.

4. ____ **Highlight** each time you use "I" in your story. If you have included it too many times, substitute a better word choice.

5. ____ **Highlight** the conclusion to your story. If there is no conclusion, add one.

Required Editing

1. ____ **Circle** a minimum of 3 words with questionable spellings. Look up the correct spelling in the dictionary and write it above the word.

2. ____ **Put a dot** under the first word in each sentence to be sure you have used a capital letter. Add capital letters where they are needed.

3. ____ **Draw a box** around the punctuation at the end of each sentence. Make sure you have used the appropriate punctuation.

Great Genre Writing Lessons Scholastic Professional Books

Questions to guide listening for PERSONAL NARRATIVES:

Listener: _____

Author: _____ Title: _____

1 What is the setting of the story? What sensory words has the author used to describe the setting?

_____

_____

_____

_____

_____

2 What are some of the main events in the story? What details has the author used to create word pictures?

_____

_____

_____

_____

_____

3 In what ways can you relate to the author's story? What connections can you make between the story and your own life?

_____

_____

_____

_____

_____

49

Phenomenal Fiction!

Fictional Narrative Writing

Selecting a Topic

Students given the opportunity to create and invent stories are engaged and motivated writers!

1. You may assign themes or "story starters" to focus students, provide a list of possibilities for students to choose from, or encourage students to choose their own topics.

2. To help students choose their own topics, have them each brainstorm three possibilities, circulate their lists, and ask for several more ideas from their peers. After gathering their "master lists," students can highlight their top three choices. Brainstorming and then narrowing topics in this way assists each student in deciding on a topic.

Pre-writing

Next, before asking students to begin writing, teach them about the elements of a fictional story and how to use a story map. Copy both story maps (pages 56 and 57) for each student.

1. Explain setting as anywhere or anytime the story takes place. In order to engage students around setting, encourage them to think of all the sensory things they might experience in their story's setting. Some questions you might ask students include: *What did it look like? What did you hear? What did you see? What were you able to touch? Did it have a particular smell?* Students fill in the setting on a sensory story map (page 56).

Possible Topics for
FICTIONAL NARRATIVE WRITING

- On a return trip from your best friend's house, you get lost in the woods.
- In the middle of a hot summer day, the weather changes drastically.
- While relaxing at home alone, your pet begins to talk.
- You get separated from your family on a vacation far away from home.
- Time travel is possible, and you may go anywhere you wish, but only for one day.
- After eating your breakfast, you shrink to the size of an ant.
- On a recent trip to an amusement park, an amazing thing happened.
- The President has you do his/her job for one day.
- A successful new product has been invented to help students with their homework and you are the first to own it.
- When you open up your mailbox, inside is a mysterious letter for you.
- A genie appears in your bedroom and offers to grant you three wishes.
- Things seemed to be going as planned on a class field trip, until . . . .
- You have a new and unusual classroom teacher for a day.

2 Once setting has been established, move on to characters. To begin, have students identify and describe a character in their story. Encourage details about a character's physical appearance, personality, likes and dislikes, talents, and unique characteristics.

3 Now have students fill in the character pieces of their sensory story maps.

4 Explain that every story needs a problem or conflict—something the characters will work to solve. Now give students time to generate a conflict for their own story, and map it with a sequence of events (page 57).

5 The last part of a story is the resolution, wherein the problem is solved and any loose ends tied up. Students can now develop their own resolution and complete their story's map.

Drafting (a)

As they begin writing their stories, students will need a lead: an interesting introduction or first impression that will hook the reader.

1 Introduce the three ways students can begin their pieces: with an action, description or dialogue. Teach students that an action lead places the reader in a scene where characters are already in motion, or doing something—and requires the reader to figure out what is happening in the story. A descriptive lead gives the reader a "picture" of the story's setting, characters, or plot and is full of juicy adjectives. The third way students can begin their stories is with a dialogue lead, which throws the reader into a conversation between two or more characters and makes the reader curious about what is happening.

2 Give students copies of pages 58, 59 and 60 and have them read them aloud. Then present model leads taken from literature and ask students to identify which type of lead is used.

3 After discussing a variety of leads, have students write different leads for their own stories. Challenge them to write one of each of the three types of leads. Have students share their options with a peer, and then choose their favorite to begin their story.

Drafting (b)

Once students have finished writing their leads, they are ready to continue with the other elements of their stories.

1. Referring back to their sensory story maps, have students begin to introduce their setting and characters to the reader.

2. Students should then write each of the main events (refer again to their sensory story maps) with specific supporting details. Tell them that their characters shouldn't solve a problem too quickly, nor should there be so many events that it is difficult for the reader to follow.

3. After writing all of the main events leading up to the solution of the problem, students will be ready to write a satisfying resolution that ties up all of the loose ends.

Revising (a)

Two ways that students can add description and "word pictures" to their writing during revisions is through the use of similes and metaphors.

1. Introduce similes as phrases that compare two different things using the words "like" or "as." For example, "The sky was as blue as the deep waters of the Pacific Ocean." Ask students to provide other similes.

2. Teach metaphors as phrases that compare two different things without using the words "like" or "as." For example, "The idea was a seed planted in her mind, watered by everything she read and growing every day," or, "The umbrella was a roof over his head, protecting him from the violent onset of rain." Ask students to provide other metaphors.

3. Provide nouns and ask students to describe each using first a simile and then a metaphor. Or, show students various pictures and encourage them to describe the images in writing. Once students have generated their own examples of similes and metaphors, they can share them with a partner. Remind students the purpose of including similes and metaphors in their writing is to paint a clearer picture for the reader.

Revising (b)

Students are now ready to revise their own writing. Pass out the required revising checklist (page 62) and the synonyms on page 61 for reference.

Editing

Using their required editing checklist (page 62), ask students to edit their narratives for correct spelling, capitalization, punctuation, paragraphing, and grammar.

Peer Conferencing

Encourage students to share their stories with a peer and elicit feedback (page 63 and 85). For some questions to guide the listening, see page 63.

Publishing

Students are now ready to publish their final copies. As a follow-up, they may want to pair up with a peer or younger buddy from another class and share their stories. You might also publish the pieces as a class book.

Additional Ideas for Teaching
FICTIONAL NARRATIVE WRITING

- Whenever reading stories as a class, revisit each of the story elements and discuss how authors have tackled them.

- As a pre-writing activity to help students generate ideas for their fictional writing, divide a chart into three columns labeled: setting, characters, and problem. Have students work in teams to generate ideas for various settings, interesting characters, and creative problems. Post each team's lists so students can refer to the charts when generating their own ideas.

- Write a collective story with students and complete a different element of the story each day. Students will enjoy creating an adventure to follow together, while you have an opportunity to model strategies and skills covered in class.

- Have students experiment daily with descriptive writing by giving them practice words for which to generate synonyms, sentences to make "show not tell," nouns to characterize using similes or metaphors, and pictures to describe. Take every opportunity to point out the clever ways authors hook readers with descriptive writing. Use some of your students' favorite authors as models.

Fictional Narrative Writing

Name _____

Setting:

sights: _____

smells: _____

sounds: _____

Character:

appearance: _____

what he or she says: _____

what he or she does: _____

what he or she thinks: _____

Character:

appearance: _____

what he or she says: _____

what he or she does: _____

what he or she thinks: _____

Character:

appearance: _____

what he or she says: _____

what he or she does: _____

what he or she thinks: _____

Problem or Conflict (what the characters will work to solve):

_____

_____

_____

_____

Great Genre Writing Lessons Scholastic Professional Books

Name _____

Sensory Story Map for Fictional Writing—2

Event 1:

sights: _____

smells: _____

sounds: _____

Event 2:

sights: _____

smells: _____

sounds: _____

Event 3:

sights: _____

smells: _____

sounds: _____

Event 4:

sights: _____

smells: _____

sounds: _____

Solution/Resolution/Outcome (how the problem is solved):

_____

_____

_____

_____

Great Genre Writing Lessons Scholastic Professional Books

Story Leads

Lead: the beginning, introduction, start,
              first impression of a story

Action Lead:

☑ the reader is placed in a scene where
  characters are in action, or doing something

☑ uses verbs

Descriptive Lead:

☑ gives the reader "a picture" of
  what is happening in the story

☑ uses adjectives

Dialogue Lead:

☑ places the reader into a conversation
  between two or more characters

☑ uses spoken dialogue

Great Genre Writing Lessons   Scholastic Professional Books

Sample Descriptive Lead

The yellow school bus slowly crawled its way down tree-lined Anderson Street. Finally, it screamed to a stop, and Agnes, our driver, pulled the door open with her knotty hands. I headed down the worn steps onto the gravel road and began my short walk home. After arriving at our two-story colonial, I yanked open our stubborn burgundy front door and headed into the living room. Anxious to finish the book I had been reading for weeks, I cleared a place on the comfy sofa. Not long after curling up and beginning to read, I heard a low grumbling sound. Goosebumps slowly slithered up and down my spine.

My blue eyes scanned the room for something intrusive. When I didn't see anything, I tiptoed across the blue shag carpet towards the staircase. Knowing the stairs so well, it was unnecessary to hold the banister as I headed upstairs. Making a sharp left at the top of the staircase, the first place I thought to hide was my parents large walk-in closet. After opening the door, I slid inside and crouched under a row of dresses. Not long after closing the door, I heard the grumbling sound coming closer—and soon the scratching began.

Sample Action Lead

As soon as the school bus squealed and huffed its final sounds, I leaped off and darted toward my house. After yanking open the burgundy front door, I ran inside and threw myself on the couch. Today was the day I would finally finish my book. Not long after beginning to read, I heard a low grumbling sound. Fear rippled through me like wind blowing across a pond.

Looking around and panting heavily, I charged up the stairs and into my parents' bedroom. Noticing that their closet door was open and realizing my time was limited, I leaped in and slammed the door shut. Not long after closing the door, I heard the grumbling sound coming closer—and soon the scratching began.

Great Genre Writing Lessons Scholastic Professional Books

Sample Dialogue Lead

"Mom, I'm home!" I yelled.

"How was school today?" she hollered from inside the kitchen.

"OK," I retorted, not really wanting to strike up a lengthy conversation. "If you don't mind, I would like to curl up on the sofa and finish the book I'm reading."

"Not a problem, I promise to stay out of your way!" my mother replied.

Shortly after beginning my journey into the wonderful fantasy world in my book, I heard a low grumbling sound and felt something soft briefly touch my shoulders.

"Mom, quit making jokes. I'm trying to finish this book!"

There was no reply and I began to panic.

"Mom? Mom!" I continued to yell as I charged up the stairs. "Where are you? Is everything OK?"

I ran straight for her bedroom and into the closet where I felt I would be safe. My screams for my mother continued, however. I began to hear the noise come closer and soon heard scratching at the door.

"Help me!"

Great Genre Writing Lessons Scholastic Professional Books

100 Savvy "Said" Substitutions

accused	added	admitted
agreed	announced	answered
apologized	argued	asked
assured	babbled	barked
bawled	begged	bellowed
blubbered	blurted	boasted
boomed	bragged	breathed
cackled	called	cautioned
challenged	chanted	chattered
cheered	chirped	choked
chuckled	claimed	commanded
complained	continued	contributed
coughed	crabbed	decided
declared	demanded	discussed
echoed	enjoyed	exaggerated
exclaimed	explained	exploded
expressed	greeted	groaned
growled	grumbled	grunted
gulped	hinted	hissed
hollered	howled	indicated
inquired	insisted	interjected
interrogated	interrupted	jabbered
jeered	joked	laughed
marveled	mentioned	moaned
mouthed	mumbled	murmured
muttered	nodded	noted
observed	persisted	persuaded
pleaded	predicted	proclaimed
promised	pronounced	questioned
rambled	replied	reported
responded	screamed	screeched
shouted	shrieked	teased
uttered	wailed	whimpered
whined		

Great Genre Writing Lessons   Scholastic Professional Books

Fictional Narrative

Required Revising

1. ____ **Label** your LEAD in the margin and **circle** a minimum of 3 words that *prove* it is that type of lead.

2. ____ **Replace** a minimum of 4 words with a "juicy" synonym. At least 1 word should come from your lead.

3. ____ If you haven't attempted DIALOGUE, put a * next to a place in your piece where dialogue would be appropriate. Insert dialogue that includes at least 2 exchanges between characters.

4. ____ **Highlight** 2 words you have used in place of "said" in dialogue.

5. ____ <u>Underline</u> the SETTING of your story. Insert 1 *simile* to describe the setting.

6. ____ **Circle** 3 nouns in your piece and describe each using a *simile* or *metaphor.*

7. ____ **Highlight** the SOLUTION to the problem in your story. If there is no solution, add one.

Required Editing

1. ____ **Circle** a minimum of 5 words with questionable spellings. Look up the correct spelling in the dictionary and write it above the word.

2. ____ **Put a red dot** under all capital letters. Capitalize all names and the first word in each sentence.

3. ____ **Draw a box** around the punctuation at the end of each sentence. Make sure you have used the appropriate punctuation. If there is dialogue, make sure the punctuation is inside the quotations.

4. ____ <u>Underline</u> what each character says in your dialogue. Make sure there are quotation marks at the beginning and end of each part you underline.

Great Genre Writing Lessons Scholastic Professional Books

Questions to guide listening for FICTIONAL NARRATIVES:

1. What is the setting of the story? What sensory words has the author used to describe the setting?

_____

_____

2. Who are the characters in the story? Who is the main character?

_____

_____

3. How has the author made the characters seem believable? What are some of the traits of any well-developed characters?

_____

_____

4. What is the problem or conflict in the story?

_____

_____

5. What are some of the main events in the story? What details has the author used to create word pictures or make you feel as if you are there?

_____

_____

6. What is some of the memorable (if any) dialogue in the story?

_____

_____

7. In what ways does the story stretch your imagination?

_____

_____

8. What was the resolution to the problem in the story? How did the author tie up any of the "loose ends" in the story?

_____

_____

Great Genre Writing Lessons Scholastic Professional Books

Clear and Convincing Paragraphs, Essays, and Editorials

Persuasive Writing

Selecting a Topic

Students will be excited and motivated by an opportunity to share their opinions on specific topics! They will learn that in order to get their readers to agree with their opinions, they will need to persuade them with convincing reasons and persuasive vocabulary.

1. Ask students to develop a list of possible essay topics. Encourage issues that students care about, and that are relevant to their lives, such as persuading a friend or family member to purchase something, do something, or change something.

2. Teachers may also choose to focus students on topics that are relevant to the classroom setting, curriculum, or interests. For example, brainstorm locations students have explored in their social studies curriculum, and challenge them to convince their readers to visit.

3. After seeing they have a number of possible options, students can choose to write about the topic that interests them most.

Pre-writing

Once students have chosen their topics, show them how to identify the argument, as well as which side they will support.

1. Students can begin by listing all of the facts or information they know about their subject.

2. After students have gathered all of the necessary facts and details, explore with them the importance of a strong argument (see right). Have them choose points they feel will best support their opinion.

3. Once they have determined the most important points, students are ready to complete their first graphic organizer (page 70).

> **Writing a strong argument is like hooking a fish.**
>
> Dropping a line into the water hoping a fish will bite probably wouldn't prove very successful. If you *really* wanted to catch a fish, you would have to add a juicy worm or maybe even a fancy lure. Writers with an opinion try to "hook" their readers. But instead of adding tempting bait to their line, they write *strong reasons* to support their opinion.

Pre-writing

Careful word selection is one of the most important components of persuasive writing. By identifying persuasive adjectives and synonyms to replace less-exciting adjectives, students will develop a bank of words that evoke feeling and emotion in the reader, and illuminate strong positive or negative responses to a specific topic (page 72).

1. Place students into small groups and assign each group an example from one of the following topics:

a place	(Africa)
a product	(electric toothbrush)
an activity	(exercising)
an invention	(high-tech sneakers)
an important cause	(saving our planet)
an event	(carnival)

2. Give each group a large piece of chart paper with their topic at the top. Have students brainstorm juicy adjectives that would persuade someone to agree with their argument about their topic.

3. After all groups have had time to brainstorm, share their lists. What you should end up with is one large bank of persuasive vocabulary words that students can use and refer to when writing their own persuasive essays.

4. To take this activity one step further, use some simple adjectives from students' charts and have them brainstorm synonyms for those adjectives in their small groups. Some adjectives for which students could brainstorm synonyms include big, small, nice, beautiful, happy, or good (page 47).

5. After identifying persuasive vocabulary, and prior to writing the first drafts of their essay, students can apply their new vocabulary in some practice persuasive paragraphs. Post some sample persuasive topics, and have students select one each. Then challenge them to complete the graphic organizer on page 71 including a topic sentence that states an opinion.

6. Once students have practice, they are ready to use their graphic organizer again, this time for their larger persuasive piece.

Drafting

After gathering all the necessary details and information to support their arguments and persuade their readers, students are ready to begin their first drafts.

1. Before students begin writing, show them several models of persuasive essays, both powerful and weak (page 73 is one example).

2 As students brainstorm the strengths and weaknesses of each essay, list their observations to use as a guide for what they should do when composing their own first drafts. Some strengths may include a strong argument, convincing details, persuasive vocabulary, a logical organization of ideas, and an overall presentation that makes the reader think and feel.

3 Invite students to begin writing their own essays, starting with a strong and convincing introduction. Advise students to begin by introducing their topic and stating their opinion. Have them develop a couple of different introductions and swap results with a classmate for feedback.

4 Next, refer students to their outlines and have them use their main ideas to write the body or middle part of their essay. Remind them that each main idea, along with its supporting details, should stand alone in its own paragraph.

5 Now, to help students prepare to write their conclusions, refer back to the topics explored in their small groups, and brainstorm effective conclusions to those issues. Emphasize the importance of restating their opinions as well as some of the most persuasive main facts. Then have students use all they've learned to write conclusions to their own pieces.

Revising ....

Pass out the required revising checklist (page 74) and have students revise their own writing.

Editing ....

Using the required editing checklist (page 74), students can edit their own essays for correct spelling, capitalization, punctuation, paragraphing, and grammar.

Peer Conferencing ....

Encourage students to share essays with a peer and elicit feedback (pages 75 and 85.)

Publishing

Students are now ready to create the formal, final copies of their essays. Once the pieces are published, guide students through self-reflecting and setting goals for the persuasive writing they will do in the future (page 86).

Additional Ideas for Teaching
PERSUASIVE WRITING

- Stretch students' creative thinking skills by having them incorporate humor into their essays. Challenge them to convince an audience of something improbable. For example, students could write about extending a school vacation, creating an unconventional new school event, or going on an unusual field trip.

- Ask each student to keep an ongoing list of persuasive vocabulary to apply to their writing throughout the year. Have them use the vocabulary from their lists to persuade you to do things in the classroom. For example, students might convince you to extend their recess by five minutes, or give them additional free time at the end of the day.

- Have students write persuasive letters to real audiences on relevant topics. For example, students might write to their school principal persuading her/him to visit their classroom and read them a story.

- Challenge students to invent a unique and useful product for their classmates, and write an advertisement persuading other students to buy their imaginary product.

- Motivate students to write persuasive arguments about where they feel their seat should be in the classroom and who they should be sitting near. Let the students know the effectiveness of their arguments will influence your decision to move or not move their seats.

- Encourage students to clip persuasive advertisements from magazines and newspapers and post them on a chart. Have them brainstorm with partners whether or not the ads are effective and convincing and why.

- Ask students to analyze an editorial from a local newspaper by defining the topic of the editorial and listing the main points or arguments made by the author.

- Have students write their own newspaper editorial wherein they choose a topic and perspective, and develop arguments to persuade the reader.

Graphic Organizer for Persuasive Paragraph—1

Topic Sentence (state your opinion)

_____

_____

_____

Reasons to Support Your Opinion

- _____
- _____
- _____
- _____
- _____

Closing Sentence (restate your opinion)

_____

_____

_____

Great Genre Writing Lessons Scholastic Professional Books

Name _____

Topic/Opinion:

Main Idea:

Supporting Details and Persuasive words:

Main Idea:

Supporting Details and Persuasive words:

Main Idea:

Supporting Details and Persuasive words:

Conclusion/Restate Opinion:

Great Genre Writing Lessons Scholastic Professional Books

Powerful Words

unquestionable

tremendous

outrageous

dazzling

splendid

magnificent

petite

ample

fascinating

eccentric

glorious

amazing

phenomenal

lively

tempting

dazzling

brilliant

tranquil

appealing

worthwhile

incredible

gorgeous

abundant

gigantic

comfortable

marvelous

generous

tantalizing

exuberant

memorable

spectacular

superb

vivid

quaint

stunning

first class

exceptional

breathtaking

quintessential

Great Genre Writing Lessons Scholastic Professional Books

Model Persuasive Paragraph

Dear Senator,

I am writing to tell you how important it is for you to protect our earth. First of all, if we don't protect our trees, beautiful birds and cuddly animals will be left homeless. Next, without plants, we wouldn't be able to gaze across the forests and see the lush, green vegetation. Most importantly, we need to protect our clear, clean drinking water. In conclusion, the trees have prevented our soil from washing away and have absorbed some of the evil poisons from the air. For all of these reasons and more, please protect our earth—it is the only one we have.

Sincerely,

Elyse Smith

73

Persuasive Writing

Required Revising

1 ____ **Highlight** your topic sentence to be sure you have stated your opinion.

2 ____ **Number** each supporting detail in your piece. Evidence should be in an order that makes sense, with your strongest supporting details first.

3 ____ **Circle** each persuasive word you have used. Add a minimum of 2 persuasive words to your piece.

4 ____ **Draw a star** next to every indentation. Indent a new paragraph every time you introduce a new main idea.

5 ____ **Highlight** your conclusion to be sure you have restated your opinion.

Required Editing

1 ____ **Circle** a minimum of 3 words with questionable spellings. Look up the correct spelling in the dictionary and write it above the word.

2 ____ **Put a dot** under the first word in each sentence to be sure you have used a capital letter. Add capital letters where they are needed.

3 ____ **Draw a box** around the punctuation at the end of each sentence. Make sure you have used the appropriate punctuation.

Great Genre Writing Lessons Scholastic Professional Books

Name _____

Questions to guide listening for PERSUASIVE WRITING:

1. What is the topic of the persuasive piece?

   _____
   _____
   _____

2. What is the author's opinion?

   _____
   _____
   _____

3. Has the author provided sufficient evidence and supporting details?

   _____
   _____
   _____

4. After hearing the piece, do you agree with the author's opinion?

   _____
   _____
   _____

5. What are some persuasive words the author included?

   _____
   _____
   _____

Great Genre Writing Lessons   Scholastic Professional Books

Additional Tools for

Tantalizing Writing!

Sentence Reminders

1. A sentence is made up of one or more words that express a complete thought.

2. A sentence has two parts:
   - subject (noun)
   - predicate (verb)

3. A sentence can:
   - make a statement
   - give a command
   - show strong emotion

4. A sentence:
   - begins with a capital letter
   - ends with a period, question mark, or exclamation point

Great Genre Writing Lessons Scholastic Professional Books

Effective Paragraphs

- ❑ have one topic

- ❑ have a topic sentence

- ❑ have supporting details

- ❑ have "juicy" words

- ❑ have complete sentences

- ❑ have sentences in a sequential order
  that makes sense

- ❑ have sentences that begin in different ways

Great Genre Writing Lessons Scholastic Professional Books

Revising Paragraphs

❑ Do the sentences in the paragraph stick to the topic?

❑ Are the sentences organized in the correct order?

❑ Are all of my sentences complete?

❑ Have I tried to start my sentences in different ways?

❑ Does my first sentence "hook" the reader?

Revise your paragraph here.

_____

_____

_____

_____

_____

_____

_____

_____

_____

_____

_____

_____

_____

_____

_____

_____

Great Genre Writing Lessons Scholastic Professional Books

Name _____

Writing Rubric

	Yes	Sometimes	No
I've answered all parts of the question being asked.	❑	❑	❑
I've stayed focused and on the topic.	❑	❑	❑
I've used details from the reading passage to support my answer.	❑	❑	❑
I've organized my writing with a beginning, middle and end.	❑	❑	❑
I've used different kinds of words in my writing and have not used the same words over and over.	❑	❑	❑
I've chosen words that make my writing clear.	❑	❑	❑

On a scale of 1–5, I would give my writing a ____ because _____

_____

_____

_____

_____

_____

_____

_____

_____

Great Genre Writing Lessons Scholastic Professional Books

Name _____

Editing Rubric

	Yes	Sometimes	No
I've used complete sentences.	☐	☐	☐
I've started each sentence with a capital letter.	☐	☐	☐
I've made sure all proper nouns begin with a capital letter.	☐	☐	☐
I've ended each sentence with a period, an exclamation point, or a question mark.	☐	☐	☐
I've followed all of the rules of grammar and punctuation that I know.	☐	☐	☐
I've spelled each word correctly using clues from the question and reading to help me.	☐	☐	☐
I've indented for every new paragraph.	☐	☐	☐
My writing is neat and easy for others to read.	☐	☐	☐

On a scale of 1–5, I would give my piece a _____ because _____

_____

_____

_____

_____

_____

_____

_____

Great Genre Writing Lessons Scholastic Professional Books

All-Purpose Rubric for Assessing _____
type of writing

Description of the task's goals:

_____

_____

_____

Scores

3 Proficient

The work product or performance achieves all goals set for the task. It is complete and indicates a very good understanding of the knowledge required to complete the task.

_____

_____

2 Satisfactory

The work product or performance achieves many of the goals set for the task. It is almost complete and indicates an adequate understanding of the knowledge required to complete the task.

_____

_____

1 Developing

The work product or performance achieves some of the goals set for the task. It is partially complete and indicates a limited understanding of the knowledge required to complete the task.

_____

_____

0 Novice

The product or response does not meet the basic requirements of the task. Although there may be an attempt to meet one or two of the task's requirements, the response is incomplete.

_____

_____

Great Genre Writing Lessons Scholastic Professional Books

Scoring Guide for Assessing _____

Description of the task: _____
_____
_____
_____

Levels of Achievement

For each key element, describe various degrees of achievement in meeting the task's goals.

Key Elements	4	3	2	1
Content	strong	appropriate	acceptable	unacceptable
Directions Followed	completely	mostly	to some degree	barely
Development of ideas	extremely strong	strong	somewhat developed	undeveloped
Editing	thorough	careful	inconsistent	poor

Great Genre Writing Lessons Scholastic Professional Books

Rubric for Assessing Writing

Name _____

Title: _____

Writing Effectiveness:	Level ③	Level ②	Level ①
Idea Development			
Organization			
Language Usage			
Mechanics			

Great Genre Writing Lessons Scholastic Professional Books

Name _____

Writing Log

Title/Genre	Date	Target Skills	Goal

Great Genre Writing Lessons Scholastic Professional Books

Writing Self-Reflection

Read your piece to yourself, then thoughtfully complete the following sentences.

I liked my piece because it had . . .

1 _____

_____

2 _____

_____

3 _____

_____

Some areas where I could improve are . . .

1 _____

_____

2 _____

_____

3 _____

_____

My goal for next time I write . . .

_____

_____

_____

_____

_____

Great Genre Writing Lessons Scholastic Professional Books

Name _____

Partner Feedback

Hand this paper to a partner. Have him or her complete the sentences below after *hearing you read* your piece and then *reading it to him- or herself.*

I liked your piece because it had . . .

1. _____
   _____

2. _____
   _____

3. _____
   _____

Some areas where you could improve are . . .

1. _____
   _____

2. _____
   _____

3. _____
   _____

_____
Partner Signature

Great Genre Writing Lessons Scholastic Professional Books

Name _____

Goal Setting Sheet

Author's Name _____ Type of Writing _____

1. Target skills emphasized in class during the writing of this piece:

   • _____

   • _____

   • _____

   • _____

   • _____

2. Goals I have for the next time I write in this genre:

   • _____

   • _____

   • _____

   • _____

   • _____

Great Genre Writing Lessons Scholastic Professional Books

Writer's Name _____

Goals/Self-Reflection

1. In this piece, did you meet any of your previously set goals?

   _____

2. If so, which ones?

   _____

   _____

   _____

3. How did you know you had met your goal(s)?

   _____

   _____

   _____

   _____

4. If you haven't met any of your previously set goals, which one(s) are you going to focus on in your next piece of writing?

   _____

   _____

   _____

Teacher Comments:

   _____

   _____

   _____

   _____

   _____

   _____

   _____

Great Genre Writing Lessons Scholastic Professional Books

An End of the Year Reflection
About Your Progress as a Writer

After reviewing the pieces in your writing folder or portfolio, write a brief piece about your growth as a writer this year. Consider the following:

- changes in your writing skills
- your feelings/attitudes about writing
- other thoughts you have about writing

In your piece, respond to each of the following questions:

1. What is the easiest part of the writing process for you now (pre-writing, drafting, revising, editing, publishing, or proofreading)? Why?

2. What can you do more easily now than you could at the beginning of the year?

3. What is the hardest part of the writing process for you now (pre-writing, drafting, revising, editing, publishing, or proofreading)? Why?

4. What are your overall strengths as a writer?

5. What are some aspects of your writing that you would like to continue to improve?

6. What is your favorite kind of writing (process writing, personal narratives, fictional narratives, informational essays and/or reports, or persuasive writing)? Why?

Proofreading Marks

Editor's Marks	Meaning	Example
═	capitalize	they visited the Grand Canyon. ═
/	make it lowercase	Ellen was late for the ₱arty.
Sp.	spelling mistake	January is the first (moth) *sp.* of the year.
⊙	add a period	Manuel plays hockey ⊙
ℓ	delete (remove)	Nick is in the (the) seventh grade.
∧	add a word	The red *car* is missing a wheel. ∧
⌃,	add a comma	He ate a banana ∧ an apple, and a pear.
∼	reverse words or letters	A whale is a (mammal sea).
⌄∧	add an apostrophe	Angels father came to the game. ∧
⌃⌃ / ⌄⌄ ∧ / ∧	add quotation marks	∨You're late,∨ yelled the bus driver. ∧ ∧
#	make a space	Alex plays the/guitar. #
⌢	close the space	The butter fly landed on the flower.
¶	begin a new paragraph	to see. ¶ Finally, I feel . . .

Great Genre Writing Lessons Scholastic Professional Books

A Word a Day

Sentence relating to me:

Synonyms:

Antonyms:

Picture to help remember this word:

Word:

Sounds like:

Variations on the word:

Definition:

Sentence relating to me:

Synonyms:

Antonyms:

Picture to help remember this word:

Word:

Sounds like:

Variations on the word:

Definition:

Great Genre Writing Lessons Scholastic Professional Books

Notes

Notes